Antigone Kefala lives in Sydney. She has taught English to migrants, and worked as an arts administrator. Apart from her poetry she has published three prose works.

To Alici and Peter
Much love
Antigone
2010

CONTEMPORARY AUSTRALIAN POETS

By the same author:

Poetry

The Alien
Thirsty Weather
European Notebook

Prose

The First Journey
The Island
Alexia

ABSENCE

NEW & SELECTED POEMS

ANTIGONE KEFALA

HALE & IREMONGER

To Anastasia, Kimon and Homer

Typeset, printed & bound by
Southwood Press Pty Limited
80–92 Chapel Street, Marrickville, NSW 2204

For the publisher
Hale & Iremonger Pty Limited
PO Box 205, Alexandria, NSW 2015

National Library of Australia Cataloguing-in-Publication entry

Kefala, Antigone.
Absence.

ISBN 0 86806 476 9

I. Title. (Series: Contempory Australian poets).

A821.3

Publication of this title was assisted by the Australia Council, the Federal Government's arts funding and advisory body

Photomontages and front cover image by Peter Lyssiotis
Author photograph by Warwick Hatton

Contents

Absence (1992)

Acknowledgements

I thank the editors of the publications in which many of these poems have first appeared: *Antipodes*, *Arena*, *Arts National*, *Aspect*, *Australian*, *Blast*, *Bulletin*, *Helix*, *Hemisphere*, *Kunapipi*, *Luna*, *Makar*, *Mattoid*, *Meanjin*, *Nation Review*, *New Poetry*, *Outrider*, *Poetry Australia*, *Scripsi*, *Southerly*, *Tasmanian Review*, and *Westerly*.

from

The Alien

HOLIDAYS IN THE COUNTRY

In dreams begins the journey, they would say
moving the candle in the darkened room
that smelt of cherry jam and basil.
I watched their shadows moving on the walls
straining to hear the corners creaking in the dark
afraid of the black night that fell outside
in silent, feathered sheets, of the abandoned
courtyard, save for the big dogs,
and far away the well.

When darkness came they talked of Katka,
of the well, in secret voices.
Put your ear to the ground, virgin,
and hear the walls groaning out of dumb mouths.
The way down cast in mica flames,
burning unheard like eyes; wild men's eyes,
dead men's eyes, glazed now in veils
upon veils of stone water.

The jump, Katka had said, would bring you
to the other shore. A land where hills and trees
are of the purest gold, where glass birds sing,
and where the air, fine powdered crystal curtains
hanging from a still blue sky, chimes in an unfelt
breeze. And you are light, shadowless, falling
upon these fields forever petrified in silence.

NEW BORN

You were not one of us
then.
Had still within your
skin the scent
of the great darkness.

Your eyes were glassy,
absorbed my own reflection
giving nothing back,
just depth, the depth
of silent waters.

Only your voice that
shrilled in night
born out of an
eternity of fear
was human.

THE PEANUT VENDOR

You see them leaning out of gates
their faces bored on Sunday afternoons
their eyes living past landscapes.
Newcomers from old countries.
The one I see each night catching the 9 o'clock.
Dark, stocky, with two beady eyes; wan now,
spare weathered face, stump of a hand,
a basket full of peanuts.

The ancient quays at home have forged him patiently
for years, so deeply and so well, that as he walks,
bow-legged, the tables sprout around him, and the sea
familiar and deceptive in the glass like silence of
the light, and everwhere, uncoiling in the air,
the plaintive voices of *amanedes*.

Yet if one spoke to him in parks, of home,
his eyes would flicker for a moment only,
past the accumulated tiredness of years,
refusing to be lured, suspicious.

The owner dead. The one who did possess in his
own youth the secret of the living bird,
and could have made it fly,
breathtakingly, blue nerve and sunlight.

FAMILY LIFE

I am tired, living at home among strangers,
sitting at the same tables,
waiting for an acceptance that never comes,
an understanding that would not be born,
the measure in us already spent.

Then I go out, in the busy streets,
and see you, young men made of for evers,
talking or laughing in trains,
unaware of the seed, already at work,
with blind hands;
and think of him,
silent now, burdened with unlived years,
walking alone in overgrown gardens,
under the rain, seeking forgetfulness.

THE MOTEL

Far down, unreal under the soft rain,
the city; in the emptiness, only the
traffic lights changed unconcerned.
At night, the room was hot,
bathed in a bluish light.
For long, the glass walls seemed to break
under the shrieks of sirens;
in the lull, the wails of the plumbing
reached from far away, then died.
Only I, waited for the silence.

Quite late, past television voices,
the shadow from upstairs would start
to measure with dull, even steps the darkness,
going over the same narrow spot,
a desperate soul, sending obscure signals
to ears much finer than our own.
Maybe, as in the ancient stories,
the thing that they had killed
to raise so high,
still had a voice.

THE ACROBAT

I am the one performing day by day
the search rites before your naked eye.
It is not you I reach for — though
I may be crying your name into the
endless desolation of the sky,
day after day, year after year,
eternities. You know it well.

I only cry in order to appease my fear.
Warm my icy limbs with my own echo.
Pretend you are not there.
Forget myself admiring my tricks.
Hold on. The effort to hold on
to this tight rope that offers no
support against the darkness.

Who will teach me not to fear
the fall?

SATURDAY NIGHT

Prophets at street corners, in neat grey suits.
Fixed eyes, unseeing, selling the old cures.
And everywhere the river,
midnight blue, flowing unheard above the silent trees
studded with magic signs.

Then we went up in our furs, in the rough foyer,
wooden horses under the stairs, 'to remind us
of our beginnings', she said patting the little dog.
The walls covered in magician's tricks,
mirrors, and the paint dead.

When the play started we grew silent.
We watched them move under the plastic lights,
inner landscapes of dust and spare parts.
The ancient masks cast now in corrugated iron.

At the end we came out empty-handed in the
narrow lanes, and down William Street,
through forests of broken walls and rubble,
so many pairs, holding hands, our gestures
no longer our own, multiplied to infinity
in windows. The world made of couples,
kissing, smiling at each other, stylised
movements following the eternal blueprint.

BOTANICAL GARDENS

Past the old trees, glass butterflies
fluttered their wings along the burning
surface of the waters.
Look at the dragonfly, you said.
See how it still holds on. Like us.
A little longer.
Only the shell was there, transparent,
full of the marvel of its hollow wings.
The fine leaves of the bamboo swayed over the lake
in the still silence, and the wings swayed too.
And on the burnished mirror that advanced
clouds travelled.
It was growing dark.

AT THE PICTURES

They had started the evening together,
waiting in their seats, the girl silent,
the boy noisy, with curly hair,
his busy hands touching her hungrily,
like a thirsty man who would never
have enough, eating her away, diligently,
absorbed, with vacant eyes.
The hunger not his, passed on,
untouched, from the beginning,
inhabiting shadows.

MEMORY

'I please those whom I most should please.'
Sophocles – *Antigone*

I

Were that enough in these strange lands.
Not even our offerings can rest,
aimless in unknown cities.
And the Gods no longer living in our eyes,
neither the ones above, nor the below,
and we, robbed of our release.

The streets were foreign in the dream.
No one but us,
and fountains in deserted squares under the rain.
At night time. You small and vulnerable,
complaining of some dark disease that emptied you.
And I afraid. Taking you in my arms as if a child.
Weightless.

And when I turned, I saw them near the fountain,
watching us. Their uniforms were blue, glazed in
the light. Then they moved in silent steps over
the gleaming pavements. Moved unheard, unruffled
in the rain, I could not see their faces.
Moved relentlessly towards us,
and I covered you with my arms and cried desperately
in the silence, my voice unheard,
cried before the black night descended on us,
my whole body cried full of the old desperation.

II

The wind would stop abruptly and the silence
would fill with moonlight, falling unceasingly
like a blue still rain over the sleeping hills,
and in the deep of night the silk tearing
sound of waves would break over the dead sand.

Then from downstairs the echo of that foreign laugh
would come, surprised and unsubstantial in the stillness,
forced out of you by those black shadows
no one could exorcize.
In the strained hollowness the walls listened.
So you coughed to assure us that the unknown
was not so menacing,
mindful of our narrow knowledge of the dark world
and our social ways.

You that had lost the image and the way,
had lost now even the recollection of the way,
and wandered through the broken walls,
in that far country,
and sometimes in a stray sunray, some meaning
of the past would come to you, in strange blue shapes,
and then before our blind eyes,
the crystal vision of the world would rest untouched.

III

Inside, past the locked doors, the corridors stretched
empty, dark. A smell of boiled peas and disinfectant.
I watched the window not to see you coming, spent,
unfamiliar,
lost in that common house, brought by a man in white.
Watched the window blinded by light, passed the man,
his shaven head cut in stone, stooped and motionless,
shedding
his marbles tears one by one; the woman crying softly.

'They steal my time,' you said in a low voice.
Then watched the floor as if my presence were too much.
And in the silence, the white men moved,
their pockets full of time, their steps so sure
cushioned by what they stole.
'They steal my time, I shall not last much longer.'
And I protested, unconvinced, for you had aged so much.
And who could say what they forced out of you
behind those walls. The essence maybe of our time,
dripping so slowly in our blood.
Maybe they stole the measure.

The trees were cut now and the road was naked.
Soft grass, cows grazing peacefully. No peace.
The garden full of people, all agony and wounds.
Ageless.
Eroded.
Sitting under trees in silence.

THE ALIEN

. . . at night I see it rising from the hollow tower
dripping with mist
this land we search for in each other's eyes
its surface steaming in the shafts of light
immersed in silence
waves that flow in me till I am filled with terror
till all the outlines of my face are lost
till all the magic of my eyes is sucked away
and I am naked
engulfed in tentacles of emptiness
dissolving

and now, I sense only these stone hands,
moving unseen, closer and closer to the grain.
Rocks shall sprout out of us and still
the light will flower everywhere impassive . . .

from
Thirsty Weather

WAYFARERS

Was this our home? We kept asking.
This orphanage overlooking the sea
white marble pillaged by the war
left barren, the grounds wasted
bird drippings on the mosaics.
Among the crippled trees
the sealed chapel
a white dove in the dawn
flying close to the sea.

The night full of sounds
the clean moon cutting the shadows
the harbour lying warm, glass trees ablaze
and then the voices
flowing out of the golden doors
through the leaves
with the smell of fried meat
the voices, ringing with
the endless desolation of the light.

THIRSTY WEATHER

I

To find our measure, exactly,
not the echo of other voices.
The present growing out of our lungs
like a flower, with a smell
that we have re-traced through our veins
some dark, secret smell
that will bloom when the hour has struck
an animal smell
reminiscent of blood
the world's scent.

Something of us must remain
in this light
that keeps on reflecting.
We have struck it with knives
and were given
the shadow of knives in return.

Fountains
fountains with springs in the air
and we, drinking our death
in small mouthfuls.

II

They were stealing your time
you unaware
walking by the seaside
your hands full of imagined scents,
while at the tables under the trees
with the fumes of the charcoals and the herbs
they were serving light, stones —
stones and light with the water.

Blood everywhere, frozen
and the wind grinding it finely
to a golden powder that settled
like down on a young face.

If only you knew
in those ordered Sunday afternoons
the clock chiming in the quiet streets
the rocks warm like skin
and the quay newly bathed, as if a body
rising from sleep, still self-sufficient,
that you had been marked.

III

Fruit vendors with cymbal voices
rang in the afternoons
through the closed shutters
and you waited
locked in the silent room
the menace seeping slowly through your veins.

Behind the glass
the hollow-eyed watchers would sit
skulls, with thin greedy hands
voices like the telegraph wires
in winter, with scooped eyes,
inexhaustible appetites.

And the country at dusk went on singing –
'Blessed Mary, Siren of the Waters,'
a chorus of women, black clad, heavy with earth,
binding their wounds in small stitch
in their windows
and you walked down, dark eyed,
the blue still flame burning unseen your marrow.

IV

In the unknown house you came bearing the
message.
They greeted you with painted faces, full of jewels
pointing as you entered — the pendulum —
an antique piece, you thought,
rosewood, smooth with time and effort,
and gorgons' heads with green eyes.

The virgin they had hidden.
They were sure of the seeds,
indestructible, they said in set voices.
And the time of forgetfulness, you asked,
you, who had always known our superfluity.
They were unaware of the terror of trees
that exhaust themselves in the giving,
and of the mirrors everywhere
blooming relentlessly, pools of white fire
unable to contain the unimagined.

V

When the gates opened you were in the ring
drinking the awful silence of the day that waited
held in the threads that stretched
between their hands like nets
your sap running unseen on the hard ground.

All fire worshippers from the beginning
full of singed wounds
and thirsts no air could cure.

This is why later you were always
drinking water from imagined springs
along the empty paths
bending and rising
rising and bending
the movement set beyond redemption.

THE PLACE

I

The place was small, full of hills,
palm trees, almond trees, oleanders,
glass flowers falling from the sky
on the ascetic hills, the bare houses.
The ancients had been there looking for copper.

Around the courtyards in the dusk
grey men in army coats
followed the leader round the ramparts.
At night after the toll, the three
would come dressed up to count the souls.

We waited there two summers.
Tall birds with upturned beaks
picked us like grain.
We moved in herds
waited with patience to be fed
drank at the water places
between the walls our necks grew longer
stretching for the night.

II

The ships, we heard, had sunk
weighed with the charity of the new world
that kept on feeding us with toys,
letters in foreign tongues
that we could not decipher.

We gave them to our silent children, onyx-eyed,
brought up on wakes for spirits that had gone
and knew each drop that added the ingredients
to the day in the appointed measure.

For them, we looked at the cross roads
to find only the sound of running water
and the dusk settling in plum coloured
over the hills
the coolness of the evening full of promise.

III

They came in spring with the great winds
the buyers
walked through the gates in groups
their marrow discoloured
their eyes ashes
gestures full of charity.

Bidders, in markets for flesh
untouched by the taste of the coffee
and the scent of the water
on the hot stones.

IV

We travelled in old ships
with small decaying hearts
rode on the giant beast
uncertain
remembered other voyages
and the black depths
each day we feasted on the past
friends watching over
the furniture of generations
dolphins no longer followed us
we were in alien waters.

THE PROMISED LAND

I

The roads were of candy
the houses of ice-cream
the cattle of liquorice.
Pretty, we said,
drinking the green air,
as in a fairy tale, we said,
eating the green water, brackish,
breathing the smoke that rose
from the greenstone hills
and the moon alone
nailed at the bottom of the sky.

II

The people carved in wood
the mark of the knife still on them
a nordic dream whittled to knick-knacks
with glass beads in their sockets
which they washed every night
in detergents
to bleach away the weight
and travel light.

We, still walking on the high seas
drunk on the light
cobalt blue falling in tinselled drops
on the verdigris statue of the queen
stout, with a night cap on
and an orb.

III

In time
the rain closed in on us
the night like a black liquid
we fell in it
travelled down through the oil
drained of resonance
while they drank it away
in the tiled tombs
with the wingless birds on the walls
heraldic birds, with long monkey hair
and blind eyes.

IV

When our eyes failed
we used our hands
to finger the light
but the bones of the dead
were not there
eaten away by the wet
rising like breath from the leaves
the feathers of birds
a plumage the colour of mud.

Others before had read all
the signs and buried the magic
left only the wild grass
pushing bold everywhere.

V

At the tables
the plastic flowers marked by flies
and the cutlery limp
they were serving our marrow
with the boiled peas
chewing it patiently with their dentures
and singing
— for he's a jolly good fellow —

The spirits of the land
which they had slain
moved in their dreams
with eyes of burning coal
the thrust of wild beasts
coming at night with the full moon
to grip them by the throat
change the course of their appetites
give them strange diets.

THE WOMAN IN BLACK

She made the sign of the cross
in front of each one
the flame of the candle flickering
in the breath of her words
which she whispered with care
lest the gods
missed the meaning.

They, at ease in their frames
complacent in their robes of
rich reds and old gold,
they gazed just above the knot of
her scarf at the street in the sun.
So bored, all of them
with this stubborn persistence
that would have them take note.

ALTER EGO

The cardinal was waiting at the corner for a bus.
Dusk, empty Sunday streets,
the Kings' Hotel embossed in phosphorescent
yellow.

He seemed so small without his gear,
the ritual gestures and the red silk gowns
now preserved in moth balls.
The brilliant upper crust that formed the man,
suave, full of a worldly vision that had learnt
to by-pass suffering, to offer eternity
as if he had the piece at home,
and cut it into measures that would suit him.

DESERTED WIFE

In black. Made of milk,
warmth of children, toys,
baskets of newly washed clothes,
sunshine, and a skin of
translucent dragonfly wings.

Living in abandoned houses,
afraid of the dark, of the past,
her guileless arms fluttering awkwardly
as those of school girls,
waving good-bye in empty country roads.

BOWLING ALLEY

Like wrestlers,
showing off their muscles to the crowd
they waited, balls in hand,
while mechanic arms,
caught, lowered, placed the game.
The smooth floors ringing.

He was shooting birds in the glass cage.
In the liquid light the bird would rise
illusive as a wave within a moving mirror,
float gently, fall in the faint click.
The man's face closed in the red burst of light.
An age that wants to kill its prey pre-packed.

LANDSCAPES

The morning bare. Speed. Distances.
The sky raining quicksilver.
The afternoon brought the bell birds
dreams of glass
chiming in the hollow of the sky
striking the metal trees.

At dusk the forest filled with
steam gliding across the trunks
that monsters had chewed patiently
to bone, scorching their leaves
so that they hung now faded
from lime claws that reached
above the line of hills.

Below the sea began,
tame and unsure, green-grey
a lake of stale sulphur
foaming at the edges where
the builders had moved in
to bear these prehistoric beasts,
their heavy concrete bodies
squatting on tin legs,
watching the sea with hollow eyes.

ULTIMO BRIDGE

By six the bridge was empty,
soot raining on warehouses,
railyards, the hotel
where we were waiting for the fixer.

The light fell gilded through
the stained glass leaving them
absorbed, all worshippers, he knew,
as he danced lightly past their beers,
his voice — echoes of strange birds,
milk stones, salt flowers, bone trees,
earth — ochre to the touch.

The gutters full of onions,
blue dusted porcelain the sky,
above the railway clock
the new translucent moon was flying.

THE DEATH CYCLE

for Kato

I

When I saw you in the new house
you were already blind,
moving with a set smile, unsure,
feeling your way among unknown things.
'He said I will be better soon'.
Trapped in this brilliantly lit
glass cage. Everything modern.
Death only, the archaic stalker,
lying in wait in undetected shadows.

II

He rang at two.
Outside the lawns stretched empty
the wind blew restless, cold and sharp
howling through cyprus trees.
I could think only that now, now
you could not hear it anymore.

III

I thought of you last night
lying alone under that barren land
blue in the moonlight, shadowless.
You who were so afraid of darkness,
of loneliness, of silence and of death.
The earth they pushed so deftly
with their forks, the men in grey,
when they finished they all sang
that man is dust and grass
and all things are of God.

I thought of you last night
lying alone under that barren land
the wind cutting the wild grass.
You wanted to be burnt like them,
trapped in narrow rooms
described in infinite details by survivors.
You only found the album in the empty house
where they all smiled in the fading light
gone all of them taking the image of
the small girl with sad, brown eyes.

IV

Then the rain came, day after day in spring,
scuttled across the empty lawns pushed by the
wind,
curtain after curtain, unceasingly over the silence,
narrowing the eyes of magpies, skinny and old,
watching the distances with timeless eyes.
Oh! The water that fell over the walls,
over the house that shrank in empty afternoons,
narrower, deeper and deeper like a wet tomb.
Our faces green, our lips musty,
our nights full of terrors,
the terrors of the darkness on which we slept,
like in a bed, unaware, on which we walked,
innocent of the future, that flowered beguilingly.
Oh darkness, be our friend! Make us not be afraid.
The water that fell greedily, the trees gleaming
full of glass bubbles in a stray sun ray.

At night I dreamt of you swimming in ditches
full of mud, and cried, voiceless to warn you.
You moved outside now, unaware of me,
in an unknown country. Fairs, where the crowd
sang, laughed with soundless voices.
Suddenly your face above the misty blue flames
of a charcoal fire, eating with greed and fear
as on your last days . . . to keep alive . . .

When I turned away, unseen, unfelt by all of you,
outside the ring of light
the night was falling in a richness of blues.
White flame tongues flickered far away, small,
lost.
The darkness alive with faceless breaths.
A curse that moved in heavy, unheard chains.

V

Pity the dead who can not rise again
to see the light
but move in darkness heavy chained
and sigh when the rain falls.

Pity the dead for the earth has no memory
and no tongue, but of trees and of rock
and they can tell their truth only
but not ours.

LABYRINTH

The coolness of fountains
a dream
in these streets of stale dust.
The past dripping soot
through the latticed windows.

At dawn
the cobbled lanes
quicken with swallows
flying low, swift
with singing voices
and the boy in white vestments
with the angel's face, walks
out of the ancient paintings
carrying the white lily
for the Blessed Lady.

CROSSROADS

I always dream of you waiting.
Waiting in strange inns
the country side hot
you there, stooped over the dark wood
listening beyond
and that seasonless wind
with no smell to its hands
ringing through the house.

MRS MACQUARIE'S CHAIR

Night everywhere
rising from the hidden depths
dyeing the oily surface of the waters.

The hill full of black beasts
their hides breathing in the dark
their limbs rubbing against each other
like wooden swords.
Far from the bridge
the metal rattled in the wind.

Our generation — you said —
crying into telephones
the distances eating our sorrows.

SUNDAY VISIT

We listened to the music,
carefully tracing the blue patterns
of the Persian rug.
Time waited, dusted, polished,
faded like the china cups.
Through the glass doors
the spring wind moved the trees;
unsettled wind,
unsure and full of boldness.

Another cup of coffee?
They had shrunk slightly
and their eyes looked dimmer.
The Greek in the next flat had died
during the winter, the poor man.
They still went for their walks,
had planted a new daphne by the wall,
watched the resilience of the new shoots
children's arms, firm, round,
shaded so slightly by blonde silky hair.
In the evenings
they returned to the old country.

FAREWELL PARTY

I *The Stranger*

Between us
lengths of void
in which the stranger moved
he travelled through the house
wearing your features
tuned the air
played on it
long chords
that rang like a bow being drawn

silk threads
your blood
turning to gossamer
only your hands
touched us
out of memories
of affection.

II *Farewell Party*

Odd figures we waited in the landscape
among the shrubs
veiled
the sun hot on the gravelled paths.
In the trimmed lanes we approached
and retreated
moths flying closer to the flame.

What temples they had built for the guest!
The waiters were in black
ran about with adequate faces.
The singer wore a cassock and sunglasses
spoke in false accents
stood at the door and shook hands
wished us a happy life.

All the cut flowers were on the lawn
lying side by side in their cellophanes
we carried them away, unwanted,
to leave the place clean
for another farewell party.

III *Eumenides*

The road went higher
among rooftops
the temple was empty
in the hollowness of the windows
black veiled women appeared
their heads outlined in the
ashen light against the chimneys.
I hit them back with the flowers
wilted now
they disappeared — came again
stubborn, stalking the game.
Why did I have to carry the burden
of all these stalks
dying in my arms
wheeled away
my shape was going from me
while I watched it.

AIRPORT

The field was black
only the glowing purple flowers
tracing a country lane.
And then it rose
powerful, riding the dark air
deeper and deeper in the cave
sucked in
till there was nothing left
but a faint flicker
the deserted platform
I, clutching my bag.

The duty shop had closed.
Eternal the blue girl
waited among the aluminium shapes.
No living thing,
the escalators moving soundlessly.

HERAKLION

Silver blue honey
the sea
the man kept dipping his oars
in the silence.

Past the old fort
the fishermen mending their nets
debris of cork on the stone.

The sea, strolled with us
a friend at our elbow
in the evening that
was raining alabaster dust
on the waters.

AT THE MUSEUM

Behind the glass
the birds drinking the sun
the scaled river caught flowing
in the deep of their throat
the curve of their breast
at watch above the line of the hills
in some dusk, eternal
that had turned them to clay
vessels for gods.

SHRINE

The square full of echoes, the fountains playing
and young, olive green soldiers posing for the
memorial photograph. The marble tobacco stained.
Like mist, the light rose from the ground.

In the dusted shadows inside, old women,
withered, black clad, wooden statues already
carved by faith moving with sturdy fingers
their mouths overflowing with the sound of
small creeks running through pebbles
relentlessly, effortlessly in the sunshine
passed the children in their white cowls
hands listlessly touching the marbled feet.

Then they all cried below the gold ceilings
cried with voices of stone
to mark the emperor's entry in the arena
and the fragile old man hurried past them
borne on his velvet throne
his bony hand fluttering in the strong wind.

SCIENCE FICTION

The wind had stopped, the dogs were silent
the moon, fine as if drawn in silver
had risen from the cliff above the waters.
We still watched
the waxy, doll-like men who wore our faces
odourless moving through the peaceful trees
the spring of their existence
willed by unknown minds
outer space, evil magicians wearing diamond eyes.

Had they, we feared,
sucked at an essence deeper than our own
and knew already secrets
that could burn beyond remembrance.

KNOSSOS

The echoes of light
travelled the slopes
with the swallows.

In the throne room, the griffins
their peacock heads raised
were waiting
in a field of white lilies
for the god, the youth
with the crown of plumed gold.

The breath of the hills
fell and rose in the silence
under the powdered sky.

EPILOGUE

We were born tired
already knowing the lassitude of the end
our limbs full of defeated moments
passing each other in the darkness
of low ceiling rooms
the walls of massive rock, abrasive,
indifferent, closing the space.
Unable to imagine futures
in these long medicinal rooms
full of staircases leading nowhere
the telephones ringing —
messages from the departed souls
that can find no rest.
Who will hear our cries outside.
Only the rain falling silently
and the closed doors
marked exit.

THE HOUR

They were killing them
with axes
the field full of night
greenstone tongues fell
from the snake trees
and the air stirred
yet there was no sound
only the wind of the axe hitting
and the body falling
and the tread of the people
preparing the blood.

They were waiting for Teiresias
and this man, whose face
I could not see,
kept showing me the vessel
rock oil, full of metal sheens
smelling of musk.

from

European Notebook

MONUMENT

A misty rain
tinted with green
steadily sifted
on the wintry trees.

The light fell ossified
through gothic windows
on carvings, standards
overcrowded tombs
the dead, buried upright
below the marble floors,
their breath
blew thinly through your bones
the chill of time.

MUSEUM

School children's voices
fell from the carved cupola
in shattered glass.

Below the heavy ceiling
the lights trickled
over the red walls,
the inlaid tables, gilded
mirrors, carved mahogany.
An ornamentation so excessive
it multiplied obsessed in
freakish shapes, polyps of
cedar, ivory monsters with a
hundred heads, enamelled eyes.

In the closed, airless rooms,
only the faces of the guards
rose silent and detached,
kingly presences of ebony.

SERVICE

In their voices, the angle of their
shoulders, this tiredness of living,
this resignation,
as if they too were peeling with time
the stucco falling off their faces
their ivory arms green with moss.

Crossing themselves in the shadows.
The servants of God in coral red
silks, marble profiles, encrusted
voices glowing through microphones,
the place heavy with gold dust
raining
over the heads of girl brides
in elaborate whites
and eyes of black liquid.

IN THE VIA DE CALZAIOLI

Eating pizzas, drinking beer,
watching each other
in the crowded mirrors.

Above the noise, suspended
in its lonely splendour,
the giant lily cast in ice
sways slightly its slim,
translucent flower arms.

WORSHIP

They ate the soil, slept with it,
the scent coursing their blood
till they were filled with earth,
took the sheep for lovers
prayed in mutilated voices,
in harsh goat tongues they sang
of rocky sites, hard winters
echoes of wind at night
in the rough trees.

The arms of the white statue
on the peak
stretching like giant horns
in the spring sun.

THE OLD PALACE

The winds blew restless
through the empty grounds,
as always in my memory,
this accursed landscape –
now orphan girls in uniform
were playing in the tall grass,
the Sunday afternoon settling
wet and forsaken over the
dove grey walls, the long façade
with all the shutters closed,
the chapel, ochre yellow,
their thin voices flickering
in the wind . . . lady . . . lady
who are you looking for . . . ?

PARISH CHURCH

Alive, she said,
the ancient saints.
Pray, and you will see
how they will step out
and the lady herself
the all blessed,
and all the others
out of the painted wood.

Now and again
a passing car disturbed
the burning heat of the day
and from the ceiling window
the gilded light
floated soundlessly down.

LOOKING TOWARDS THE SEA

She was on the balcony
like her mother
looking towards the same
wet sea.

The place full of ruins
coal loaders, people with
furrowed faces, ravaged eyes
sweeping the peelings.

GODDESS

The evening was falling
on the porcelain dust
that moved on the waters
the milky white breath
of the goddess with snakes
who travelled below
her slim arms outstretched
poised at the centre
a secretive smile
on her listening mouth.

At her feet
the octopus waited
watchful
with eyes of the deep.

FAMILY

The garden full of trees in bloom
spring scents, angelica, birds
crying in the still, clean light.

In the dark house behind the shutters
they were waiting
with the bread and the olives.
Marble dusted, ancient faces
with eroded eyes,
shell eyes of statues bleached by time.

At night, their shadows
on the white washed walls
breathing in silence
the scent of the white lilies
blooming in the moonlight
as if consumed with longing.

RETURN TO THE GREEN COUNTRY

I

The place had shrunk
it looked cleaner, trimmer
but as empty,
the hills brooding below
the grey fermenting clouds.

The light washed in this
sea of greens, the green of
caterpillars, worms, snails,
undergrowth, dead leaves,
moist, secretive greens, and
the land watched morose
stubbornly grazing the soft rain.

II

At the station
the wind blew icy
through the rusty sheets
beyond the tracks
the washed rocks
gargoyles
in the muddy green sea
and on the hill
the house squinted, one-eyed,
behind the giant now
pohutukawa tree.

III

He smiled out of faded brown eyes,
absent-minded, searching again
through all these objects covered
now by dust, the starting point
he had lost, surprised, lamenting it,
forgetting, going back again,
a fragile thread that kept on winding
and unwinding, spinning a cocoon
of gestures from the past,
while through the tattered curtains,
past spiders in soot
covered nets, the night
crouched massive at the window,
its marble water eye
searching obsessively, yet slightly
uninvolved, the other presence
in the house,
invisible under the light.

Outside
the hills closed in a ring
of blackness,
far, far away, a lighted cage
burnt, illusive, fading,
its breath wiped out slowly
by the night.

CONFERENCE AT COLLEGE

At drinks
we approached
aimless all of us
and unknown.

The dinner long
we talked
like fish gasping for air
in a sea of noise.

I left early
past the open passages
dark fields, the lights
smokey yellow flowers.

And in the narrow room
paper brown cows
kept smiling at me
from the ceiling.

INDUSTRIAL CITY

We drove towards the city
past carcasses of cars
rotting in treacle by the
roadside, giant chimneys
topped by puffs of cream,
the black dust raining
on a landscape
that no longer cared.

At night, the railway clock
struck stubbornly the hours,
the room groggy with heat,
dogs barked furtively at the
new moon, out in a humid sky.

The first train left at dawn
the whistle marking slightly
the low sky, bleached blue
above a sea of moonstone.

SCHOOL HOLIDAYS

Brilliant copper brown cows
with monumental heads
munching the air
the sky, metal blue grey.

The carriage empty
only the girl
travelling with her mother
sensibly dressed
her blue, forget-me-not eyes
raised to the window unseeing
setting down in her diary
in childish hieroglyphics
her unformed soul
still searching for a shape
in which to rest.

THE PARTY

The guests moved restless
caged under the sky
the strong wind swept away
the music, but the beat
came back to slap your face
with the sea air.

The hero came quite late
sniffing the air
his face like a skinned animal
eaten by maggots with ice heads
a musty smell about him
as he danced
his hollow eyes turned inward,
bleak tunnels with no end.

BARBECUE

At our back
the forbidden house
and beyond
the convent on the hill
massive red.

The streets deserted
only we in the bald yard,
with the gum tree
fanning itself nervously,
eating raw meat laced
with black flies
drinking the parched wind
and making polite conversation
while the light poured on us
sizzling.

FREEDOM FIGHTER

A freedom fighter, she said
lighting the gas stove.
In the mountains we fought . . .
great days . . .
the words stubborn
weary in the shabby kitchen
with the yellowed fridge
and the tinted photograph
of the dead husband.
The house full of morose
rooms suffocated with rugs.

We came out on the low verandah
her heavy stockings pitch black
the rough spun dress the
indigo blue of some wild flower
the Sunday neighbourhood still asleep.
Come again, she said indifferently,
watching the windy street
and the Town Hall squatting
on its elephant legs,
come again.

BEER GARDEN

The man
kept attacking the steak
as if a live animal
liquid ice
running on him
through the sparse
greenery.

Outside, the heat
brushed against us
with fur hands.

DINNER

The lights exploded
on her high cheek-bones
her platinum blonde hair
the opalescence of her skin.

Her water eyes
travelled from far away
beyond her head, a sea at night
under a waning moon.

MOTHER'S STORIES

Youth

He keeps on walking slowly
through the years
always in afternoons
in early summer,
leaning on her arm.

He sang, the day he died.
He sang as if the rivers of
his blood were full of fire
as if the roots in him
were fighting in the wind
the marrow of his bones
had become sound.

Going Back

In the half-light there was only
dust, seeping slowly through
closed shutters
the faded marks of frames on the
bare walls, the thinning carpets.

At night, her voice came
beating within the walls
struggling to get out,
an agonising dumbness
faint groans that reached
as from a sea bed,
lost at the centre, each
layer robbing it of sound.

I rushed to touch the wall
and cried – Speak Mother –
there was a sigh then
that released the house
it crumbled in a golden light
behind the glass wall
far away.

INHERITANCE

Trying to hide
the nakedness of your death
from their eyes
you, who are already travelling
beyond us, indifferent.
Have you a message for us?
We are in need.

High ceiling rooms
with oak doors, dark parquetry,
closed smells.
My sealed tomb
travels in my dreams.

LITTLE DEATHS

I

The light went off in the house
I turned anxious
walked down the empty lane
silently the vortex of the night
rolled out
swiftly, rushing through the wall
pulling me in
suffocated by waves that rang
as if the void was sounding
their hot breath on my face
while I fought, wild to free myself,
something was falling
falling through black space
that echoed
in the bottomless pit.

II

In the end we reached the river.
Nothing alive but dragonflies
darting in stillness.
Autumn it must have been and the
companion was no longer there.
But you had come.
Is there no hope for us?
I asked in a small voice
worn thin by the great fear.

The echo came down with the rain,
your shadow melting slowly
falling in stripes
over the aluminium river
faster and faster
till there was only mist
and all around me, the voices
unseen, struggling
through the suffocating whiteness.

WAITING

I have set my life aside
placed it in the shade
of the familiar room
where it waits speechless.

My other self moves now,
laughs in the morning light,
watches the twilight, indigo,
remote, ungrasped,
the faint memory of a sensation
that has stirred in me sometimes,
gone now,
vanishing with the evening.

DIVINER

I

You walked above the landscape
to avert the fires,
but when you centred
you held the place
made distances grow out of it
in long stone waves.

Your lizard hands
secretly touching the light
stirring unheard in the trees
avid hands, inwardly folding
tighter and tighter
unopened lids of buds.

II

The garden on a hill
in a rocky country
the light modest
I did not know you at first
silent boy
with the defenceless mouth
through the glass
you were kissing the lips
they were moving
some breath that came from below
bringing its secrets.

THE WANDERER

The river
moved further away
in the heat of the road
shimmers of water
towards the horizon.

The salt
which they gave him at home
he would place on his tongue
to taste his own roots
and draw comfort.

The world
made of a matter that never
forgets, a symmetry so exact,
fatality at the heart
of each thing.

SUICIDE

This timelessness
that rises out of the earth,
the rocks, the sea,
envelops us, tantalizing,
a familiar yet forgotten scent
that tries to wake
lost images in the deposits
of our mind.

This silence,
the ease that fills the trees,
a promise of such bliss
of self forgetfulness.

FAMILY HISTORY

Satin in Mother's room,
mirrors, alabaster boxes,
Black Sea shells, water singing,
I went around the bed chanting:
Do you hear the sea inside me?
Stopped at the new cot
oyster head, crayfish tail,
as in the zoology books,
I picked it up and swallowed it,
horrified,
yet the thing had no taste.

When I found myself I was weeping,
beating the ground with my fists,
the wet nurses were there,
all in grey, and his face
with the dark handsome eyes
slipped away from my reach.

COMING HOME

What if
getting out of the bus
in these abandoned suburbs
pale under the street lights,
what if, as we stepped down
we forgot who we are
became lost in this absence
emptied of memory
we, the only witness of ourselves
before whom
shall the drama be enacted?

LAMENT

This voice in us
still so plaintive
that will not cease to cry.

The night brings them
the eyeless people
thin with large skulls
the odour of the void
on their breath
a parched ground
that eternally thirsts.

Absence

NIGHTS

I

The brittle sounds
of this slow agony
that searches
for a smaller
smaller safety
in the night.

The urgency that
beats against the walls
as we shrink slowly
fold over slowly
lower ourselves
into the ground.

II

The hollow of the boat
piled with bodies
wrapped in white.

Now, you
were being lowered down.
I kept calling you,
struggled to reach you,
the heaviness of all this white,
but I could find no stairs
just nails
hauling myself up
nails now bolted to the sky
suspended
on the backbone of the emptiness.

III

You had come out of the house,
in the silent street
were riding on a trolley.
The night full of menace.

You had come out of the house,
the white bear
was waiting on the chimney.
The night was full of menace.

You had come out of the house,
the white bear
was howling at the moon.
The night full of menace.

Then it leapt. The trolley vanished
with the sudden winds, the noise of
space, the blackness that was
falling, a thick, heavy liquid.

IV

We were searching for the killers,
but they were after us,
they took out their binoculars,
placed them at their eyes,
somersaulted on them,
they fired,
a thin trickle of blood
over the sand
the beach planted with pews,
a toy glass house that began
to grow, enlarge, to fill with
water, with the sound of waves,
this giant glass box, golden now,
as if of polished wood.

ABSENCE

I

The coffin arrived
full of polished brass
then the priest
giving instructions.
The first
bent down and kissed it
but the second
kept eating earth from
the golden top of the coffin
munching it
I could see straight
into the cavernous mouth.

II

Then from this height,
greater than I imagined,
they threw me in.
The water heavy
with no feel to it
just this fear on all sides,
the waves held in the air
solid marble
glossy in the ashen light.

I was swimming in a sea
of tombstones
as far as I could see
the surface crowded with
these frozen waves
tombstones to the horizon
ambushed by lifeless bodies
floating in the night.

III

Heavy with time.
Time now made of lead.
Time now made of silence
voracious
feeding on the past.
Time now made of fire.
Time now a suffocation
whistling in your veins.
Time now a chill
a fever that invades the air
ignited liquid
you sink in unsuspecting
and you drink with greed
hoping for a release.

IV

Constantly searching
in these underground rooms
to find you
to reach you
to tell you something.
The rain falling, falling
in grey metal sheens.
Inside, at the stone tables
the same shadows waiting,
speechless,
drinking at the source
of the black light.

But from the ground, unfolding
silently its secret message,
the red tulip, alive,
closing and opening its lips.

V

The air was full of voices,
of lament,
the face of a young woman kept
flashing on the giant screen.
I jumped in the deserted ring,
wings were sprouting at my back,
growing, unfolding
with a mechanical sound.
Yet all was in vain
I kept stretching my hands
but could grasp nothing,
just light, waves of light
flowing through my fingers
insubstantial.

VI

You were calling me today
the echo floating
above the muted colours
of the dawn
my name, transparent silk
moving
over the hushed colours
dipped in silence
out into a far away resonance
travelling through space.

TRANSFIGURATION

Underground. The shadows
crowded in the room.
Then light began to pour
from the arched ceiling,
exploding light
in which they danced
jumped up to touch it
and be made of light,
the light
a rain that they were
splashing in, their hands
reached upwards
bathed in these splinters
of white glass.

CHORUS

In the white shimmer
they were dancing
holding each other
one step towards
the centre, one away
shifting imperceptibly
yet static
figures on a frieze
seen from below
petrified waves
at the edge
of the abyss.

NAMELESS

I

You are the resonance
in the fanatic colour
of the sky
intoxicating light
that fans over the sea
a heavy cloth of shimmering
white gems on the horizon.

Excesses of a terror
that can never be appeased.

II

To reach you
we would dissolve into
your incandescence
pool of white fire
flood
the folded strangeness
of the night
in shafts of steaming
crystal dust
see for the first time
the magic of the earth
rise in the brilliant air
singing.

III

Speak to us.
Speak of the fire rivers
cooling in our blood.

Help us to rise
weightless
and not to grieve,
the journey, an unbinding
that knows of no return.

CHANT

Marked
by the silence of this land
I drink it again and again
sink
in this ocean of stone
in this ocean of light
the embrace of the trees
absorbed
in the shafts
of the invisible presence.

Marked
by the silence of this land
I drink it again and again.

CRAB DREAMING

They came in through the walls
that night.
They came in through the floor
rose from the open book
broody, in their muddy green shells
their armour-plated hands
kneading the air, the current
in their mouths, a muffled sound
that I could not decipher.
Was this their place?
In the feverish night
what had they come to tell?

HORSELESS RIDER

Your touch
scorched their limbs
so you drank them
drained them
to appease this thirst
this avid emptiness
that went on
scooping you away
leaving you hollow.

BROLGAS

Lithe with bronze hair
bronze skins, bronze eyes
they were dancing
stalking on awkward
elegant, thin legs,
moving their beaks
uttering dry sounds
in the eeriness of the bush
their arms, wings now
folding slowly
with a dislocated grace.

FOREST

When the car stopped
the silence
fell suddenly on us
heavy
invading the place.
Far up, the lamenting
cry of a bird
resonating,
the hum at the crest
of the trees.

LONGING

This longing
I have treated with weariness
watching you obsessed with
a stubborn, impersonal need,
skin exercise that passes
leaves no mark.

Guarding your self intact
while we waste away
fine dust over the landscape
under the awesome light.

KISS

Your face
as you bent down
emptied of you
absorbed inwardly
at some fixed centre
far away.
Obsessions
greedy elements
with unbroken wills
feeding on us.

LETTER

I think of nothing but you.
I re-invent obsessively
your presence, day by day.
I see nothing but you,
your lips constantly moving
without sound,
I bend over the silence
trying to grasp
the secret resonance.

I wait at the window
the night
still with moonlight.
Why have you left me
this unwanted luggage?

VARIATIONS ON A THEME

I

We came together silently
searching for the land
trying to find the place
struggling for it
with each other,
to allow this anguish in us
to be born.

We fought with it, body to body,
desperate ourselves
to reach the river
the flowing that would lift us
into the sunlight,
a fight to death, our eyes closed
listening to the voices inside
that were still far away
somewhere at the centre
faint echoes along dark tunnels
everything moved towards
this release that was coming
despite us
following ancient laws, inexorably.

II

We left our eyes at the door
the burn
went through our skins
strangled our breath
groped our hands
we moved in a hushed silence
sleepwalkers touching.

Later
we reached the warm lake
the water live
we floated weightless
in a cocoon of light.

SONG

I long to find you
in the uncertain silence
of my evenings
when darkness comes
and when the streets
are desolately empty
when nothing speaks
only my need of you.

TOWARDS AN ABSOLUTE PRESENT

I

You were at the window
looking at the sea
held in the glowing sunset
a petrifying emanation
that stretched to the horizon
past the islands.

II

Smaller and smaller
vanishing
in the milky air
your chair suddenly empty
a transparent shape
thrown across it, floating,
a thin light that flickered
a faint beat.
I brought out your clothes
began to dress you in a hurry
you filled out
and were very pleased
pressed my hand warmly.

III

We have assumed your tempo
wait with candour
empty vessels
to be filled with present.
But the present that comes
is self-sufficient, sheds
constantly the everyday
this useless burden.

A door. We stop undecided.
The mystery of every room.
What are we searching for?
We ask about the past
a story we have not heard
before, surprised at the
remoteness of the characters.

THEY ARE STILL COMING

I

They are still coming
coming at night to take me away
and I run out of the lighted house
down empty streets, dogs barking,
whistles, leather voices of men.
I run pushed by a panic so strong
that I see my shadow fleeing
before me, white and transparent
in the moonlight.

Yet I am running with another
a companion, shuffling in his rag-
covered feet, his long black coat
his shadow gigantic in the search
lights, and I whisper to him
hoarsely in the dark
run . . . run . . . they are coming.

II

At dawn we are still moving
paralysed in a white light
over marshes, between thick
fleshy stalks, the menace
everywhere, suffocating
rising from the ground
pressing from above
tighter and tighter.
No wind.
Just the companion, silent,
faceless, crunching through
the weeds, weighed with
this speechless suffering
the burden of these deaths.

FOLKLORE

I

This bare house, the light
apricot on the walls
and the people.
The black cat moved possessed
through the rooms
it rushed out
stopped at the two mounds
cried in a human voice — Vasili!
The sun darkened
the earth rocked
a hand reached out of the ground
the head, the body covered
in a raincoat.

They all hurried from the house
noisy, and came to him
he sat up, smiled,
not dead, they said,
they brought him the child and
there was a lot of rejoicing.

II

I met them on a country road
at the end of settlements.
In town the streets were
narrow, steep, the houses
of terracotta, the colours
of fire, the people unknown.
At the gate we saw the name.
The place was cool, starched
they were burning incense.

But the child had vanished.
We searched for it in vain.
'Don't worry,' said the woman,
as she set the table,
'it sometimes goes away . . .'
and it was in front of us
on the white table cloth
this golden insect
filigree wings stretched out
turning in death
faster and faster
as I watched unnerved
and the woman
kept pouring the soup.

FRIENDS

I

He had not changed
still his corroded self
full of self mockery and wit
sitting
on the edge of the chair
made of nails
looking sheepishly
from the corner of his glasses
under them
with a dejected face.
All of us wounded people
stubbornly
analysing the condition.

II

He was waiting for us at the pier
distant and full of courtesy
underscoring all experience,
sure of the futility of things,
a natural state, at ease in it,
yet challenging it all the time
inviting you to challenge it
coming back to it as to a favourite
state, nursing it in his arms
with the scent of tobacco and
his blue eyes, unobtrusively.

CEREMONY

She came up the stairs
in the thin white dress
with flowers in her hair,
unseeing
splashing through
the milky afternoon.
This exquisite fear
that advanced on all sides
a sea
to which she could not
give herself.

AFTER THE READING

The cage of his body
as I held it
the resonating chamber
of an instrument
still vibrating
with the last chords.

OLD NEIGHBOURHOOD

You who longed
to be held
in the palms of the world
transformed
into a timeless offering
gone
nothing left
but the emptied house
listening to the wind
and the street
with the elderly sisters
dusting their windows
polishing the evergreens.

AFTERNOON TEA

The scent of orange blossoms
intoxicating on the wind
the open road
the spring around us
rushing through the windows.

He was still there, in the house.
The silver pot, the cattle dog,
a frosted patina of dust on the
old furniture, the ornate frames,
the books.
He watched us with vague eyes
the distancing politeness
they acquire with old age.
Hot tea and biscuits,
even the past emaciated now.
'Do come again,' he said,
'and don't leave it too late.'

We drove away through the long
alley of fir trees, their cones
the desiccated wings of birds
ash grey, heavy on the ground
in the wet coolness of the evening.

DINNER

Power
had an erotic scent
he was exhilarated by
its touch, its presence,
in the candle light
his dark eyes made of agate
glittered
with a static persistence.

OLD PHOTOGRAPH

In the dusty street
looking with some unease
at the baby, the camera,
the innocent line of the
dress, the strong light.
At the back, the old car
and the cottage, tilting
on its unsteady legs.
'Our youth,' you said,
'never aware of it,
while we had it.'

THERE

There
we praise God for all things
the bread, the day, our hands
our narrow graves.

There
as the olive trees bloom
in the powdered light
our bones turn into gravel
lie in the narrow lanes
where the blind youth
with the luminous eyes
and the silent mouth
was tortured by soldiers
to disclose
the land's inheritance.

FLYING

The narrow space crowded
full of tired, faded people
with thinning hair
in dark blue suits
shuffling restless
caged animals munching nuts,
drinking, watching each other
with stale eyes.

Later
we went down
in a field of diamonds.

THE CELEBRITY

Pink, with a moon face
he waited on the dais,
half smiling through
his two front teeth,
watching us avariciously
from the funnelled depths
of his small eyes.

Then he began to talk
in a falsetto voice.
The crowd was quiet,
waiting patiently,
hoping to see the divine
promises come true.

DOCUMENTARY

We were watching
the phenomenon of his life
already old, in Venice
in the humid, opal light
his face
the washed out aftermath
of an obstinate energy
an obstinate worship,
the fanatic absolute
that had now
turned against him.

THE PLAY

The prince
was very nervous, drank his
life at speed, to see it dry.
A methylated flame burnt in
his eyes, a savage energy
that was ready to erupt,
singe his pale skin.

The courtiers
were out in the streets
groomed in the latest image
pink shirts
black leather boots
limbs made of steak
fried eggs and beer.

When the Town Hall clock
struck twelve
the daughter
of the Lord Chamberlain
went past, smiling discreetly
at her image in shop windows.

BRASS CONCERT

Votive offerings
the horns
wait under the stage lights
burnished beings
rising wet out of a gilded sea
self-contained
no regrets to mar
the perfection of their form.

TOURIST BUREAU

Past the glass doors
the statue of Aphrodite
and the fragments of gods
resting in the perfection
of their ease
he was sitting
self-contained and subdued
dreaming
of the soldier and the girl
in the coffee shop by the sea
the table with a rose
and the soldier dancing alone
a *rembetiko*
the juke-box singer
with the broken voice
calling out
. . . where are they selling hearts
so I can buy you one . . .

BLOOD

In the metallic light
the pavements
were rivers of blood
flooding the gutters
this hot, transparent liquid
made of silk
live, breathing on the stone
trying to defend itself
from the invisible killers
that were watching
watching this magnificence
this red flowering
shrinking, freezing
vanishing into the ground.

AUTUMN

The light
a subtle poison in the blood
so still
so self-contained
holding itself
upwards.

We sink
into this brittleness
as if
our only reassurance.

GROWING OLD

Growing old
with the flower sellers
in Martin Place.

This everyday — our only thing
this everyday — what happiness
this everyday
thinking of friends that are
going, against their will,
who rise to the occasion of
their illness, of their death,
matching it.
Death that is coming
in this everyday
sweetly, unseen in the light.

Growing old in these streets
gathering this knowledge one
does not want, one can not use,
a useless knowledge that
repeats itself.
The same ashen faces,
the same fear
voices over the telephone
talking of soups
in this everyday that continues
to unfold in our absence.

New Poems

THE COUPLE

They were sitting
at the empty table
with the starched table-cloth.
In the light of the window
his eyes flared up
fierce explosions of blue
the eyes of a night creature
phosphorescent in the dark.
Extinguished as he turned.
She touched his arm then
and he laughed
as if splashing in water
a release
that excited him
but of which
he was slightly afraid.

STRUGGLES

1

This fear now
repetitive, docile
a lacklustre fear
a fear with no future
the night full of eyes
suspended
in the ruins of houses
over pits of white ash
then the bombs falling
shaking the place
phosphorescent panic
out of a green sky
and we running, running
through unknown cities
unknown neighbourhoods
to reach the place.

2

I was holding a baby in my arms
the roadside full of sand
blue flowers
highwire fences
the massive shapes of chimneys
and far away the sea.

Emptiness. Only the man
in black, his eyes
glass disks, dark mirrors
cracked as he turned
the splinters falling
on the sea wall, beyond it
in the liquid light
they were lying asleep
side by side
on a bed of white pebbles.

3

On top of a dark mountain
talking to a shadow
that comes out of me
stands beside me
fluid, shimmering black.
Indifferent as I look out
the other talks of going.

It finally divides from me
slides down
rocks all the way
further and further down
it falls in silently
the heavy velvet surface
closes with no trace.

THE ACTUAL PLACES

The actual places
of these terrible events
these calamities,
the killings, the blood;
the actual places
grounds sacred for a
thousand years,
subdued now
silent and mysterious
a few modest hills
some trees, silver green
flickering in the light.

THE RIDE

Death
riding in the car
with them
touching her sister's arm
paralysed now.
Death
waiting at checkpoints
watching the landscape
through the window
while they were running
frantic
to find a salvation.
Death
riding back with them
holding her
empty now.

GUIDED TOUR

He talked relentlessly
of history, an index
of small incidents
as we walked fast
in the thin drizzle
past the palace
and the park
with the Peking ducks
the bed of daffodils
meticulously carved in yellow.

The cathedral
crowded with tombs.
In the ivory air
the arches were rising
the delicate ribs
of a body ascending
floating
above the candelabras
that blossomed
into their white
transparent fruit.

TOURISTS

As the bronze doors opened
we rushed in. The church,
a vast, dusty tomb
that echoed with the waves
of a long vanished sea.
The ornate ceilings pouring
gold, angelic blues over
the alabaster statues
ivory relics laid in porphyry
the crystal steams in icy whites
and petals of blood orange.

We moved in groups
pushed by the same need
to find
proof of our existence
proof
that we had been here
measured ourselves with the place
left a mark on it
forever.

RITUALS

The audience
knelt in silence
while the voice
came modulated through
the microphone
as if a whisper
my body . . . and my blood . . .

Then they got up
respectfully
rushed forward
to touch the mystery
to drink the mystery
came back
weighed
with this eating
of the divine.

STORY

The distances I have to cross
to meet them. They watch me
from afar, in secretive ways.
In their eyes, my angular face
caught in glass. They break
under the impact. Scattered
chips over the pavement.
The smell of fear for days.

Then they gather them slowly
melt them to make other bubbles
which they slot into place.
Better than new, they all say,
rubbing their hands.

PARABLE

There was Death
carved in stone, in the temple,
waiting, aloof, all seeing.

There was Death
in the Medicine House, incredulous
of such hopes
laughing in the dusty twilight.

There was Death
at the Traveller's Inn, serving
the food, flames of burning oil
and the sound of bells.

There was Death
in the crowd, listening
to the blind singer
songs of seeing, songs of longing.

THE COMEBACK

He appeared on the balcony
after the victory
with his new wife, young, blonde.
He tall and very thin, in grey,
his head, a skull just covered
with some parchment.

He watched the crowd
unsteady on his feet and vague
sent them awkward kisses
with his bony hand,
the wife's hand on his shoulder
guiding him.
When he spoke
his voice hollow, rasping
some over-used rhetoric from his past
in which he still believed.

CHRISTMAS DINNER

They were both waiting
slightly stiff in their ease
in the impeccable apartment.
Around them images of country
houses, diplomats in China,
uncles in astrakhan coats.

They were still quoting
Bismarck—not a nationality
but a pastime—
they found him full of wit
political incisiveness.

We listened to old carols,
admired the Christmas tree
with the glass angels,
the ancient silver set, saved,
lying exhausted on the table
crushed by ornamentation.

Outside, in the hot night,
the cicadas spun their
metallic threads, tireless
into the empty streets,
the air full of the scent
of frangipanis.

FAMILY FRIEND

The last time I had seen him
he seemed arrested
preoccupied with some inner
sound, afraid to make
full use of himself.
Still debonair
but now transparent looking
in his cafe-au-lait suit.
He drove us round the bay
that night, after the party
all of us singing.

Below the bald, sturdy hills
the small cottages   fast asleep
only the traffic lights
and our voices
carried through the windows
to the sea below
in the empty, windy night.

CONSOLATIONS

I

You were in bed.
A narrow wooden bed
tucked in neatly.
Are you all right?
I kept asking. You nodded.
I sat on the edge
I held on to the cover
to your body inside, warm.
Why are you here? I thought
and not at home
when the house is so empty.

II

Someone was giving birth
the place was full of people
I waited in the corridor
trying to place myself
then they began to call me
I rushed in
it seemed I had already lost
the vital message
the room was now a lake
the surface throbbing
with white light
a child's head was rising
from the waters
and your voice
near
calling my name.